:: HARMONY ::

A simple and systematic Treatise on the Harmonization of Melodies and Basses,

BY

T. KEIGHLEY, Mus.Doc., F.R.C.O., etc.

Professor of Harmony in the Manchester College of Music; Lecturer on the Theory of Music and Singing, and Examiner for Degrees in Music in the University of Manchester; sometime Examiner for the Royal College of Organists, Trinity College of Music (London), and the Incorporated Society of Musicians.

EXTRACT FROM PREFACE.

" In this work the Harmonization of Melodies and Basses is taught on the method used for many years at the Royal Manchester College of Music. The method is simple and systematic. From the first lesson the student is taught to think of Chords and their effect when used in the harmonization of melodies."

" Among the chief features of the work are (1) the explanations given concerning the higher discords (9ths, 11ths, and 13ths), and (2) the chapter on Applied Harmony."

Demy 8vo, in Cloth, Price FIVE SHILLINGS net.

Graded Harmony Questions and Exercises.

By T. KEIGHLEY, Mus.Doc., F.R.C.O., etc.

The object of this work is to provide a systematic course of study in a convenient form. In Books I. to IV. the exercises are arranged on the plan which has proved so successful in connection with the Author's Rudiments of Music Exercises (in " A New Manuscript Book ").

The chief features of Books I. to IV. are :—

(1) Together with each question a space is prepared for the answer (This arrangement saves time for both teacher and pupil.)

(2) The questions are carefully graded and so arranged as to lead the student to the essential features of each harmonic progression.

(3) The exercises deal with the Harmonization of Melodies, Figured Basses and Unfigured Basses. Also general exercises are given.

The Exercises in Books I. to IV. are specially suitable for candidates preparing for the L.R.A.M. and A.T.C.L. Examinations, and for all other examinations which include a knowledge of Elementary Harmony.

The Exercises in Book V. include Melodies for Voices, Melodies for Strings, Figured Basses, Unfigured Basses, Modulation Exercises, General Exercises, and First Lessons in Composition.

Book V. is specially suitable for candidates preparing for all examinations dealing with Advanced Harmony, such as A.R.C.O. ; F.R.C.O. ; A.T.C.L. ; L.T.C.L. : L.R.A.M. ; Mus. B. ; etc.

In Five Books, Royal 4to, Price ONE SHILLING and SIXPENCE each net.

LONDON—BAYLEY & FERGUSON—GLASGOW

FIRST LESSONS IN COUNTERPOINT

FIRST LESSONS

IN

COUNTERPOINT

BY

THOMAS KEIGHLEY

LECTURER IN THE UNIVERSITY OF MANCHESTER

AND

PROFESSOR OF COMPOSITION

IN THE ROYAL MANCHESTER COLLEGE OF MUSIC

BAYLEY & FERGUSON

LONDON : 2 GREAT MARLBOROUGH STREET, W.

GLASGOW : 54 QUEEN STREET

NOTE

THE author has had in mind the preparation of this little work for some time. He feels that there is a certain want of clarity and terseness in most of the books dealing with counterpoint, and though he cannot hope to have solved every student's difficulties he trusts that the average beginner will herein find considerable help.

The work deals with Simple Counterpoint and Combined Counterpoint up to the standard required by the A.R.C.O., and kindred examinations. But even for more advanced work there would be little to add, as relaxation of rules should not be indulged in until the student is writing in seven or eight parts.

Further, whilst exercises on Rudiments and Harmony have been carefully graded and fully treated by many writers, very little has been done in that direction for the student of counterpoint.

The Five Books of Exercises published in conjunction with *First Lessons in Counterpoint* are an attempt to meet this great need. The author's first idea was to publish the Exercises only, but so many points required explanation that the present book became a necessity.

The author hopes eventually to issue a work dealing with Double Counterpoint, Canon and Fugue.

CONTENTS.

INTRODUCTORY

KNOWLEDGE OF ELEMENTARY HARMONY

1. The student who desires to begin counterpoint should have a knowledge of elementary harmony, including triads and their inversions, unessential notes, suspensions, diatonic sevenths and simple modulations.

COUNTERPOINT.

2. Counterpoint is the art of adding melodies to a given voice part called the **Canto Fermo,** or *fixed song*. The **Canto Fermo (C.F.)** begins on either Tonic or Dominant, and ends with the progression Supertonic to Tonic :—

A few authors occasionally end their Canti Fermi with the progression Leading-note to Tonic :—

This is done with the idea of modernising the study of counterpoint.

3. In technical exercises there are five ways of adding a counterpoint to the Canto Fermo ; these five ways are called the **Five Species.**

The first four species are pattern-writing ; they are a preparation for the fifth species.

FIRST SPECIES.

4. The **First Species** of counterpoint, often termed " Note against Note," has notes equal in length to those of the C.F.

(*a*) With **C.F.** in semibreves :—

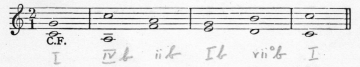

(*b*) With **C.F.** in crotchets :—

SECOND SPECIES.

5. The **Second Species** has two notes against each note of the C.F. (except the first and last notes).

Occasionally an exercise in this species has three notes to one of the C.F.

(*a*) With **C.F.** in semibreves :—

(*b*) With **C.F.** in minims :—

THIRD SPECIES.

6. In the **Third Species** there are four notes against one of the C.F. (except the first and last notes).

Occasionally an exercise has six notes to one or even eight notes to one.

(*a*) With **C.F.** in semibreves :—

(*b*) With **C.F.** in crotchets :—

* Concerning the leap of a diminished 5th, see Section 28.

FOURTH SPECIES.

7. For the **Fourth Species** the counterpoint is in syncopation :—

(*a*) With **C.F.** in semibreves :—

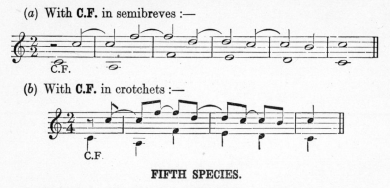

(*b*) With **C.F.** in crotchets :—

FIFTH SPECIES.

8. Though the **Fifth Species,** or **Florid Counterpoint,** is a combination of the first four, the rhythm is best when no species but the third is used complete in any bar ; and no two consecutive bars should have the same rhythm.

We give an example with the **C.F.** in semibreves :—

CHAPTER ONE

FIRST SPECIES IN TWO PARTS.

AVAILABLE INTERVALS.

9. The following Harmonic Intervals are available :—**Perfect Concords :** Unison, Octave, Perfect 5th.

(i) The Unison is used only on the first and last notes.

(ii) In counterpoint the Perfect 4th is treated as a discord.

Imperfect Concords : Major 3rd, Minor 3rd, Major 6th, Minor 6th.

THE BEGINNING.

10. The **First Note** of the C.F. will be either Tonic or Dominant, and the **First Note** of the counterpoint must form a perfect concord with it :—

At (b) it would be unwise to begin with a 5th below the C.F., as the key would seem to be F major :—

Not good.

THE CADENCE.

11. In the **Ending** or **Cadence** the C.F. proceeds from Supertonic to Tonic ; the counterpoint must have Leading-note to Tonic :—

Should the student come across a C.F. ending with Leading-note to Tonic, the counterpoint would have Supertonic to Tonic; the progression at (c) is also possible :—

SUGGESTIONS.

12. At this stage a counterpoint book is usually overburdened with rules. The student is told "Thou shalt not," until in despair he is inclined to ask, "What may I do?"

But the teacher may with advantage allow the pupil to try a few exercises, pointing out :—

(1) The counterpoint must be melodious.

(2) Contrary motion is desirable.

(3) Imperfect concords are preferable to perfect concords.

(4) Consecutive 8ves and 5ths are forbidden. "Hidden" or "exposed" consecutives must receive attention.

(5) The laws of melodic progression (such as the avoidance of the leap of any augmented interval) are to be observed.

(6) The student must aim at producing musical results.

The student's work is certain to contain some of the forbidden progressions; these may then be explained by the teacher.

We give two examples of **First Species** counterpoint :—

Each C.F. should be worked twice : (1) with counterpoint above and (2) with counterpoint below. Students must learn to transpose the C.F. into suitable keys.

AVAILABLE TRIADS.

13. Where 6 is marked in the above examples a first inversion is implied; the others are triads in the root position.

Only root positions and first inversions are used ; the second inversions are not available.

In the major key the positions are :—

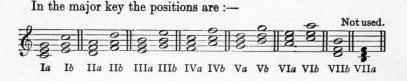

Ia   Ib   IIa   IIb   IIIa   IIIb   IVa   IVb   Va   Vb   VIa   VIb   VIIb   VIIa

And in the minor key :—

Ia   Ib   IIb   IVa   IVb   Va   Vb   VIa   VIb   VIIb

* The **diminished triads** are used in the first inversion only.   The root positions are not allowed :—

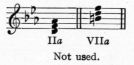

IIa   VIIa
Not used.

The **augmented triad on the mediant** is not used at all :—

IIIa   IIIb

EXERCISES.

14. The following Canti Fermi may be used for the exercises :—

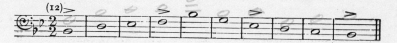

At (11) and (12) the accented bars are marked. When a Canto Fermo is given with only one semibreve in a bar the student should try to find the accented notes ; the last note is always on an accent.

COMPASS OF VOICES.

The **compass of voices** must have attention. In each exercise the student should have a particular voice in mind, and the compass of that voice is not to be exceeded. The various voices have approximately the compass given below :—

THE C CLEF. ALTO AND TENOR STAVES.

As soon as possible the C clef should be introduced. Many leger lines are thus saved, and also the student gradually acquires the ability to read string quartet and orchestral scores. Both the Tenor and Alto staves are part of the Great Staff of 11 lines; the sign always represents Middle C, the 6th line of the Great Staff :—

GENERAL RULES.

15. With a little help from the teacher a student often makes surprising progress on the lines indicated above. The rules may now be studied more closely.

FORBIDDEN CONSECUTIVES.

16. Consecutive 8ves are forbidden. If they were used, as below, the counterpoint would simply be copying the C.F., and the music at that point would cease to be in two parts :—

17. Consecutive 5ths are forbidden; they are more or less ugly in effect :—

Modern composers often use consecutive 5ths with fine effect. Students must "go through the mill" and write according to rule until they are ready to compose; the rules will then become their servants.

HIDDEN OR EXPOSED 8ves AND 5ths.

18. Hidden or **exposed 8ves and 5ths** are allowed when :—
{ (1) The triads involved are primary triads (I, IV and V); *and*
{ (2) The higher part moves by step ; thus :—

Between different positions of the same chord " exposed " 5ths or 8ves are quite good :—

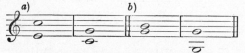

CONSECUTIVE 3rds AND 6ths.

19. Consecutive 3rds or **6ths** sound well, but if they are used too freely the counterpoint becomes a copy of the C.F. at another part of the scale. Not more than three (in short exercises not more than two) 3rds or 6ths should be used consecutively :—

Similar motion is permissible, but contrary motion is often preferable.

B

OVERLAPPING AND CROSSING.

20. Overlapping and **crossing of parts** should be avoided in two-part writing :—

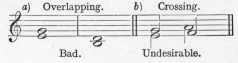

a) Overlapping. *b)* Crossing.

Bad. Undesirable.

THE LEADING-NOTE.

21. The Leading-note should not be doubled.

CHORD PROGRESSIONS.

22. Effective **chord progressions** are necessary if the counterpoint is to be really good.

Roots rising a 4th (or **falling a 5th**) are generally good if both chords are in root position. Even when inversions are used the effect is usually good.

But VII*b* to III*a* or III*b* should be avoided :—

(a *b)* *c)*

Good. Good. VII*b* III*a*

Not Good.

23. Roots rising a 5th (or **falling a 4th**) are also good ; care is occasionally required when inversions are used.

The progression VII*b* to IV*a* or IV*b* is not good :

Not Good.

a) Good. *b)* *c)*

VII*b* IV*a* VII*b* IV*b*

24. Roots rising a 3rd or **falling a 3rd** are generally good if both chords are in root position ; triads III and VII require care.

In the inversions care is necessary :—

a) Doubtful. *b)* Not Good.

I*a* III*a* VII*b* II*b*

Roots falling a 6th are the same as roots rising a 3rd ; and so on.

25. (*a*) **With roots** rising a 2nd the progressions IV*a* to V*a*, V*a* to VI*a*, and VII*b* to I*a* are good.   The inversions need study ; thus III*a* to IV*a* is bad ; III*b* to IV*b* is good.

Occasionally the first chord may be inverted and the second in root position :—

(*b*) With **roots falling a 2nd** the progression VI*a* to V*a* is good. In all other progressions the second chord should generally be inverted, regardless of whether the first chord is in root position or its inversion :—

THE TRITONE.

26. (*a*) There is danger of **the false relation of the tritone** when the progressions involve triads III and IV, or IV and V :—

(*b*) The bad effect comes from the Leading-note in the upper part and the Subdominant in the lower part, *with both parts moving by step of a 2nd.*

(*c*) When either part moves by an interval greater than a 2nd the effect is acceptable :—

(*d*) The notes forming the interval of the tritone are not to be used as the highest and lowest notes in any melodic passage :—

The notes forming the interval of an augmented 4th are three tones apart ; hence the term TRITONE.

THE REPETITION OF A CHORD.

27. The chord on a weak beat should not anticipate that which occurs on the succeeding strong beat :—

(1) At (*a*) the bass part has the same note on consecutive strong beats ; this should be avoided.

(2) Triad VII*b* is really a part of the dominant 7th. Therefore, in the progression V*a* (or V*b*) to VII*b*, triad V must occur on the strong beat :—

MELODIC INTERVALS AVAILABLE.

28. The available **melodic intervals** are :—

By conjunct movement—Major and minor 2nd (according to the diatonic scale).

By disjunct movement—

    (*a*) Major and minor 3rd.

    (*b*) Perfect 4th and 5th.

    (*c*) Minor 6th.

    (*d*) Perfect 8ve.

    (*e*) Diminished 4th and diminished 5th.

(i) Some writers do not allow the diminished 4th and 5th.   When these intervals are used the voice-part should return one step, thus :—

(ii) The following leaps are not allowed :—major 6th ; sevenths ; augmented intervals ; any interval greater than an 8ve.

(iii) Chromatic semitones are not available.

LEAP OF A LARGE INTERVAL.

29. The leap of a minor 6th or an 8ve should be preceded and followed by a note within the interval :—

The Leading-note must not leap an 8ve.

ARPEGGIOS.

30. (*a*) **Arpeggios** are not usually good :—

(*b*) After **two successive leaps** in the same direction the part should return :—

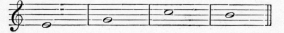

(*c*) **Two successive leaps** should not form a 7th, unless the three notes involved form or are part of a minor 7th (particularly the dominant 7th) and the 7th is properly resolved :—

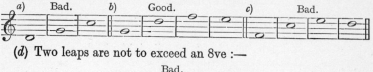

(*d*) Two leaps are not to exceed an 8ve :—

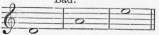

CONJUNCT MOVEMENT.

31. Continuous conjunct movement is bad ; judicious leaps add vigour to the counterpoint :—

DISJUNCT MOVEMENT.

32. Excessive disjunct movement is too unstable :—

TAUTOLOGY.

33. Weak repetitions (or tautology) must be avoided :—

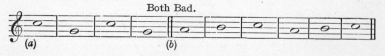

REPEATED NOTES.

34. The **repetition of a note** should be avoided when the counterpoint is in the bass ; even in the upper part the repetitions are undesirable, and on no account must a note be given three times :—

Such repetitions are best when the first note is on an accent :—

CHANGE OF KEY.

35. Modulation is rarely necessary in a short exercise, and need only be used when the C.F. either definitely changes key or strongly suggests a change.

SUGGESTIONS FOR MINOR KEYS.

36. In exercises in minor keys there is often a brief transition to the relative major key. This may be taken freely.

THE MINOR 7th OF THE MINOR SCALE.

37. But a change of key is not necessarily denoted by the **minor 7th of the scale.**   When this note occurs in a descending scale passage it may be harmonised as the root, 3rd or 5th of a triad.   In all such passages the next note but one should be part of the dominant chord :—

Key A minor.

At (*a*) G is the root of the chord ; at (*b*) G is the 3rd ; the 5th of a triad cannot be used in the bass.

At (*a*) F is the root ; at (*b*) the 3rd ; at (*c*) the 5th.   Whenever the minor 7th is treated in any other way a modulation to the relative major is implied.

THE MAJOR 6th OF THE MINOR SCALE.

38. Also, in the minor scale a major 6th which is ascending to the major 7th may be harmonised as the root, 3rd or 5th of a triad :—

Key E minor.

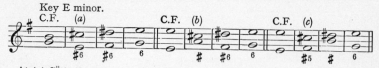

At (a) C♯ is the root ; at (b) the 3rd ; at (c) the 5th.

With the major 6th in the bass only one position is possible :—

Key A minor.

The student should try to solve this question :—" Why cannot the major 6th be used in the bass as the root, or as the 5th of a triad ?"

(1) Dim. chord in root pos? (2) 6/4 not allowed.

39. In two-part writing the following effect is quite good :—

Key A minor.

But in three-part writing there would be difficulties. The chord at (a) could only be :—(i) the second inversion of the triad of A ; *or* (ii) the first inversion of the augmented triad on C. Neither chord is allowed :—

Because of these complications many writers refuse to accept the progression in two-part writing.

CHAPTER TWO

SECOND SPECIES IN TWO PARTS

FIRST AND LAST BARS.

40. In this species the counterpoint has two notes to one in the C.F., except that :—

  (i) Against a C.F. in semibreves the first bar begins with a minim rest, followed by a minim on a **perfect concord,** exactly as detailed in Section 10 :—

  (ii) The last bar contains a semibreve (either unison or perfect 8ve) :—

When the first note of the C.F. is a minim or a crotchet the counterpoint must agree :—

FIRST NOTE IN EACH BAR.

41. Throughout the exercise the **first note** in the bar must be a **concord** (perfect or imperfect), as explained in Section 9.

SECOND NOTE IN EACH BAR.

42. The **second note** in the bar may be :—

(i) A concord, approached and quitted quite freely :—

(ii) A passing-note, approached and quitted by step :—

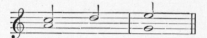

This is useful when the minims on successive beats are a 3rd apart.

(iii) An auxiliary note :—

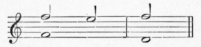

The auxiliary note may be used when the minims on successive beats are on the same note.

THE CADENCE.

43. (i) The following cadences are accepted by all authors :—

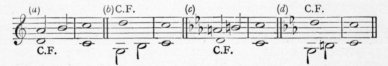

The above are in accordance with the view that the *last note but one* of the counterpoint should be the leading-note. In the author's opinion the examples at (b) and (d) should be allowed in this form :—

Two reasons will suffice :—First, in the *First Species* it is generally accepted that imperfect concords are preferable to perfect concords ; and secondly, in the *Second Species* the first note in each bar is more important than the second note. These facts favour the use of the leading-note as the first note in the examples (b) and (d).

(ii) The following is permitted by such writers as allow the leap of a diminished interval :—

C.F.

This is not available below the C.F.

EXAMPLES.

If the student has grasped the simple facts stated above, exercises may be worked on the Canti Fermi given in Sections 14 or 53. Each C.F. should be worked twice, thus :—

C.F.
V*a*   I*b*   I*a*   II*a*   II*b*   I*b*   II*a* VII*b* I*a*

C.F.
V*a*   I*a*   VI*a*   II*b*   II*a* IV*b* III*b*   V*b*   I*a*

(a) Here there is a change of chord ; see Section 47 (ii).

(b) The cadence is in accordance with the note to Section 43 (i).

ADDITIONAL RULES

THE UNISON.

44. The **unison** may be used in the first and last bars, exactly as in the first species ; it may also be used on the **second minim** in any other bar :—

The leading-note must not be doubled either at the unison or 8ve.

TWO VOICES A 2nd APART.

45. When an unessential note forms a 2nd with the C.F., the **two** parts should not move in similar motion :—

Contrary motion only after a 2nd.

Bad.

Also, the second should not be succeeded by a unison :—

Bad.

THE INTERVAL OF A 7th.

46. A major 7th formed by an unessential note may rise one step, but a minor 7th should follow its natural tendency and fall one step :—

a)   Good.   *b)*   Good.   *c)*   Not Advisable.

CHANGE OF HARMONY.

47. (i) The **second note** in a bar may be approached by step and quitted by leap. This implies a change of harmony :—

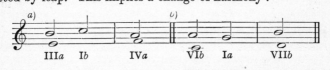

IIIa   Ib   IVa   VIb   Ia   VIIb

The leap in such progressions should be in the opposite direction to the previous conjunct movement :—

Not Advisable.   Good.

In many passages the second note may be regarded either **as a** passing-note or a new harmony note (as explained above) :—

But in the following the leading-note is strong enough to imply a change of harmony; this must be correctly followed :—

(ii) The following progressions are good :—

These should be avoided :—

At (c) the effect is too much like a $\frac{6}{4}$.
At (d) the second minim should be quitted by step.

THE TRITONE.

48. The tritone does not exist in such passages as the following :—

The C at (i) and the B at (ii) are unessential notes.

CONSECUTIVE 5ths AND 8ves.

49. (i) Consecutive 5ths or 8ves with the C.F. may neither occur between the first minims of consecutive bars :—

nor between the second minim of one bar and the first of the next :—

(ii) Consecutive 5ths or 8ves may occur between the C.F. and the second minims of successive bars provided both these minims are not (*a*) the highest or (*b*) the lowest in each bar :—

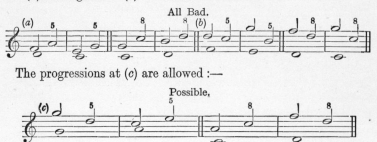

The progressions at (*c*) are allowed :—

(iii) Such passages as the following are not objectionable ; in each example the 5th marked * is formed by an unessential note :—

REPEATED NOTES AND THE LEAP OF AN 8ve.

50. Repeated notes are forbidden :—

But the leap of an 8ve is good, provided the rule given in Section 29 receives attention :—

THE MINOR 7th OF THE MINOR SCALE.

51. (i) The minor 7th of the minor scale may be freely used as a passing-note, ascending or descending :—

Key C minor.

Or as an auxiliary note :—

(ii) Authors generally fight shy of using the minor 7th as a harmony note. But as the progressions in Section 37 are accepted the following should not be rejected, seeing that the minor 7th virtually proceeds to the minor 6th :—

Key G minor.

Such passages as the following are modulations to the relative major key. They are out of place at the beginning of an exercise, but may be used after the original key has been established :—

Key G minor.   Key B♭ major.

THE MAJOR 6th OF THE MINOR SCALE.

52. (i) The major 6th may be used as an ascending passing-note on the way to the major 7th :—

Key C minor.

(ii) As a descending passing-note, provided the chords are V*a* to V*b*, or VII*b* to V*b* :—

Key C minor.

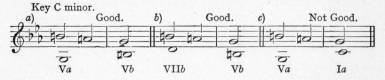

(iii) Or as a harmony note on the way to the major 7th of the scale :—

Key C minor.

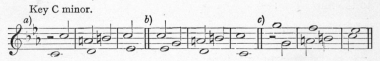

In Section 51 we used the Second Species in accordance with the progressions in Section 37. Likewise the major 6th should be allowed, provided the conditions laid down in Section 38 are observed, as in the following :—

Key E minor.

Here the major 6th virtually proceeds to the major 7th.

The progressions at Sections 51 (ii) and 52 (iii) are logical developments of the First Species progressions. But they are probably risky for examination work.

EXERCISES.

53. (*a*) Add a Soprano part in the Second Species to the C.F. given below :—

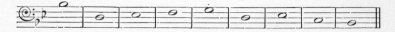

(*b*) Transpose the above C.F. into the key of D, writing on the Treble Staff, and add a Bass in the Second Species.

(*c*) To this C.F. add a Bass part in the Second Species :—

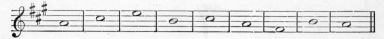

(*d*) Transpose the above C.F. into the key of C. Write it on the Bass Staff, and add a Soprano part in the Second Species.

(*e*) Each of these Canti Fermi should be used in two exercises, as described above :—

CHAPTER THREE

THIRD SPECIES IN TWO PARTS

54. The counterpoint now has four notes to one of the C.F.

FIRST AND LAST BARS.

55. (i) The first bar begins with a crotchet rest. The first note must be a perfect concord.

(ii) The last bar contains a semibreve (either 8ve or unison) as in the First and Second Species.

THE FOUR NOTES IN A BAR.

56. The first note in each bar must form a concord (either perfect or imperfect) with the C.F. The other notes may be :—

(i) Diatonic passing-notes, approached and quitted by step :—

or (ii) auxiliary notes (used on the second or fourth crotchets, but not on the third) :—

or (iii) harmony notes, which may be taken or left by leap :—

THE CADENCE.

57. The following are used :—

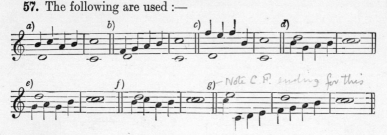

(i) The changing notes at (*a*) and (*f*) should rarely be used except in the cadence. And care must always be taken, when changing notes are used, that the 3rd crotchet does not anticipate the 1st crotchet of the succeeding bar :—

(ii) The progression at (*c*) would not be used except by those who accept the leap of a diminished 5th.

(iii) The following are good ; but they are not accepted by authors who insist on having the leading-note as the last note but one of the counterpoint :—

58. The student may now write a few exercises in the Third Species, using any of the Canti Fermi in Sections 14 and 53. At present the C.F. should be written in semibreves.

Later the rules and recommendations given below must be studied.

RULES AND RECOMMENDATIONS

CONSECUTIVE 8ves AND 5ths.

59. (i) Consecutive 8ves may not occur between any note of one bar and the first of the next :—

(ii) Consecutive 5ths are also to be avoided :—

When the first 5th is an unessential note, the progression is often possible :—

(iii) Some authors permit the following because there is a change of chord at * :—

(iv) The 8ves or 5ths should not be the highest or lowest notes in successive bars :—

CHANGE OF HARMONY.

60. The harmony may occasionally be changed once in a bar. The change is best on the 3rd crotchet (some authors accept a change on the 2nd or the 4th crotchet) :—

ARPEGGIOS.

61. (i) The four notes in a bar should not form part of one harmony :—

3 notes in arpeggio are allowed, as in next example.

(ii) The leap of a major 6th should be avoided. Some authors also object to the leap of a minor 6th.

(iii) The 5th of a chord may be used in the Bass part, arpeggio fashion, provided the root of the chord is not sounded above :—

In all such progressions the 5th of the chord must move either (1) to the root or 3rd of chord, as at (*a*) and (*b*) above, or (2) proceed by step, as at (*c*).

UNESSENTIAL NOTES.

62. (i) When two passing-notes are used in succession the voice must proceed in the same direction until a harmony note is reached :—

(ii) After a scale passage the voice should not leap in the same direction to an accented note :—

(iii) Step-wise progression from the 5th of a chord up to the root is good when the 7th from the root is major. Should the 7th be minor, as at (*c*), care must be taken that the succeeding notes satisfy the ear :—

(iv) A 2nd should not be followed by the unison ; nor should the voices proceed in similar motion from a 2nd :—

Bad.   Bad.

THE NOTA CAMBIATA.

63. The Nota Cambiata may be used :—

(i) When the first and fourth notes are concords :—

(ii) When the first note is at the interval of a 6th and the fourth note is a discord :—

Authors differ considerably on these points. Some condemn the example at (ii) above.

THE MINOR KEY.

64. The minor 6th and 7th, or major 6th and 7th, may be freely used in accordance with the principles expressed in Sections 37, 38, 51 and 52.

CROSSING OF PARTS.

65. In two-part writing crossing of parts is undesirable.

THE LEADING-NOTE.

66. The leading-note should not be doubled.

GENERAL RECOMMENDATION.

67. The counterpoint should have a fairly wide range and a good melodic curve, with scale passages and leaps nicely balanced. The following is an example of how not to do it :—

In the above the counterpoint does little more than wobble round the chief harmony notes.

68. Each C.F. should be worked twice :—

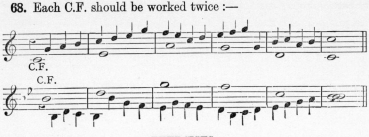

EXERCISES.

69. (a) To this C.F. add a Treble part in the Third Species :—

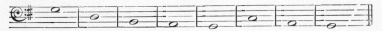

(b) Transpose the above into the key of E, writing on the Treble Staff, and add a Bass part in the Third Species.

(c) To this C.F. add a Bass part in the Third Species :—

(d) Transpose the above C.F. into the key of B minor, writing on the Bass Staff, and add a Treble part in the Third Species.

(e) Each of these Canti Fermi should do duty for two exercises :—

CHAPTER FOUR

FOURTH SPECIES IN TWO PARTS

70. In the Fourth Species syncopation is used. The first bar contains a minim rest and a minim :—

(i) The counterpoint must begin with a perfect concord.

(ii) In bar 2 a *suspension* is used :—

    (1) is the note of preparation.

    (2)   ,,   ,,   suspension (a discord).

    (3)   ,,   ,,   resolution.

(iii) In bar 3 the note B is a harmony note ; it is therefore free to leap to another harmony note.

SUSPENSIONS IN THE UPPER PART.

71. When the syncopated note forms a discord it should descend one step to a concord. The available suspensions are :—

(i) The 9 to 8 (but the 2 to 1 must never be used) :—

(ii) The 7 to 6 (*i.e.* the first inversion of the 9 to 8) :—

(iii) The 4 to 3 :—

Some authors object to the 4-3 suspension above the subdominant. But if the tritone is avoided (see Section 26 (c)) the progression should be accepted :—

(iv) The progressions 6 to 5 and 5 to 6 may be either suspensions or syncopated concords :—

If the progression 5-6 is to be regarded as an upward suspension it must only be used with leading-note to tonic as at (b) above, or mediant to subdominant as at (c).

i.e. rising a semitone

SUSPENSIONS IN THE BASS.

72. The suspensions now available are :—

(i) The 2 to 3 :—

(ii) The 4 to 5 :—

(iii) The 5 to 6 :—

The 5 to 6 and 6 to 5 must often be regarded as syncopated concords. The progression at (c) cannot be a syncopated concord ; it should be avoided :—

73. (i) The unison may be used on the second beat of the bar :—

(ii) When syncopated, the leading-note may be doubled on the first beat of the bar :—

(iii) The following progressions, allowed by some authors, should be avoided :—

74. The syncopation should not be broken except in cases of necessity.

75. Cadences :—

76. Examples :—

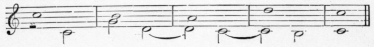

77. The following Canti Fermi are suitable for the Fourth Species :—

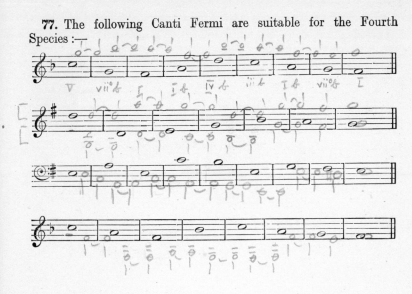

CHAPTER FIVE

FIFTH SPECIES IN TWO PARTS

78. In the Fifth Species (often termed florid counterpoint) the other species are freely combined.

(i) Also, quavers may be introduced, though not too often. Only two quavers in one bar should be used ; these are to be on the weak beats (2nd or 4th crotchets), and they are to be approached and quitted by step :—

(ii) The Fourth Species may be used in the ordinary way, or with ornamental resolutions :—

At (*a*) the usual resolution is given ; at (*b*) the counterpoint leaps to another note of the chord before resolving ; at (*c*) two quavers are used ; at (*d*) the voice leaps down a 3rd and then returns to the harmony note ; at (*e*) and (*f*) a step upwards is taken before the true resolution ; at (*g*) the procedure is exactly as at (*d*).

In all these examples the actual resolution occurs on the second minim of the bar, as in the ordinary form at (*a*). But the note of resolution may be a crotchet :—

The following are faulty :—

Care is always necessary when the ornamentation is above the suspension, as at (*e*), (*f*), (*j*) and (*k*).

79. In the first bar of an exercise any of these may be used :—

A quaver entry as at (*a*) should never be used, and many writers object to the form at (*b*), though in the author's opinion the latter is good :—

THE CADENCE.

80. In the cadence a suspended discord is often the best :—

The Third Species forms may be freely used :—

(See Section 57 for more examples.)

Or more florid forms :—

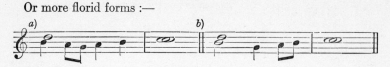

81. The various species should be mixed in florid fashion within the bar. The Second and Fourth Species are not to be used in their simple form :—

The Third Species may occasionally be used :—

A free intermixing should be got :—

(i) A minim which is preceded by quicker notes in the same bar must be tied over to the next bar, as at * above. (But the Cadence is not included in this rule. See Section 80.)

(ii) The second of two tied notes may be either a minim or a crotchet.

(iii) Two tied crotchets should not be used.

(iv) When the Nota Cambiata is used (see Section 63) the first note must be tied to a minim of the previous bar :—

(v) Auxiliary notes on the third crotchet are not advisable :—

(vi) Some writers object to a passing note on the third crotchet in bars with mixed notes :—

But with four crotchets in a bar there is no objection :—

(vii) The Fourth Species, whether resolved ornamentally or not, should not be used for more than two consecutive bars.

(viii) A passage including eight crotchets (even if varied with quavers) would be better spread over three bars than confined to two bars :—

Possible.   Not Advisable.

(ix) In two parts a dotted minim should be avoided :

(x) The second minim of a bar should not be an unessential note :—

(xi) The same rhythmic figure should not be used in two successive bars :—

82. Example :—

Exercises should now be written on the Canti Fermi previously given.

N.B.   (i) Each exercise should contain two or three examples of syncopation.

(ii) The Handelian *Amen* figure is very useful, either (*a*) direct or (*b*) by inverse movement :—

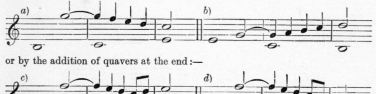

or by the addition of quavers at the end :—

(In combined counterpoint these are particularly helpful.)

CHAPTER SIX

SIMPLE COUNTERPOINT IN THREE PARTS

FIRST SPECIES IN THREE PARTS.

The Beginning.

83. (i) The first chord must be in root position. One of the added parts will form a perfect concord with the C.F. ; the other part should be the 3rd of the chord :—

The Cadence.

(ii) When the C.F. is in one of the upper parts the penultimate chord must be the dominant, either in first inversion or root position :—

With the C.F. in the bass the penultimate chord is the leading-note triad in the first inversion :—

(iii) The final chord is always to be in root position.

General Recommendations.

(iv) The counterpoints must be melodious, and complete harmonies should be used when possible.

(v) The rules of harmony concerning parts moving in similar motion should be observed.

(vi) A note should rarely be repeated.

(vii) In three-part writing the parts may cross in order that melodic interest may be obtained, though it is rarely advisable to cross parts with the bass.

Example :—

See Section 28.

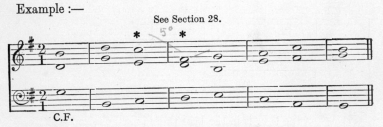

C.F.

The student should now write exercises in three parts. Each C.F. may be worked three times, (a) in bass, (b) in inner part, and (c) in treble.

SECOND SPECIES IN THREE PARTS.

The Beginning.

84. (i) Against a given C.F. one part will be in the Second Species, the other in the First Species.

(ii) The first two notes sounded together will form a perfect concord (see Section 10), therefore the Second Species may now begin with the 3rd of the chord, even when it is in the bass. This will apply to all counterpoint in three parts :—

C.F.

D

The Cadence.

(iii) As in the First Species (see Section 83) when the C.F. is in one of the upper parts, the penultimate chord will be the dominant, either in root position or first inversion :—

See Section 43.

Or the cadence may be borrowed from the Fourth Species :—

(iv) When the C.F. is in the bass there is less choice :—

Lengthy exercises are to be avoided in the early stages. A C.F. of 6 or 7 notes, worked in the six possible ways, will give the student an idea of the difficulties.

Thus :—

1st	{	C.F. 1st Species. 2nd Species.		2nd	{	C.F. 2nd Species. 1st Species.
3rd	{	1st Species. C.F. 2nd Species.		4th	{	2nd Species. C.F. 1st Species.
5th	{	1st Species. 2nd Species. C.F.		6th	{	2nd Species. 1st Species. C.F.

Examples :—

* See Section 43.

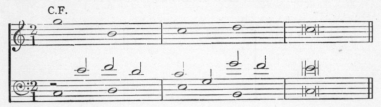

THIRD SPECIES IN THREE PARTS.

The Beginning.

85. (i) The first two notes sounded together must form a perfect concord, but the first note of the third species may be the 3rd of the chord, even when it is in the bass part (see Section 84).

The Cadence.

(ii) Greater variety is now possible :—

The Leading Note.

(iii) The leading-note may occasionally be doubled on the **2nd** crotchet :—

But on the 1st, 3rd and 4th crotchets the effect is undesirable :—

(iv) In a scale passage the leading-note may fall :—

Examples :—

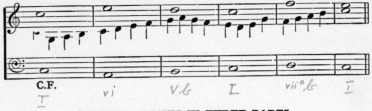

FOURTH SPECIES IN THREE PARTS.

The Beginning.

86. (i) The Fourth Species may begin with the 3rd of the chord (see Section 84) :—

The Cadence.

(ii)

General Observations.

(iii) A fourth in the upper parts may be sounded against a suspended discord :—

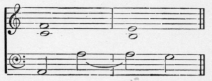

or against a suspended concord :—

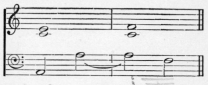

(iv) In this species there is often great difficulty in obtaining complete chords.

(v) When the suspension is in the top part it is not good to have the inner part a 9th below :—

i.e. do not sound the note of resolution in another inner part.

The progression may occasionally be allowed when the inner part moves by step in contrary motion :—

Examples :—

FIFTH SPECIES IN THREE PARTS.

87. Examples :—

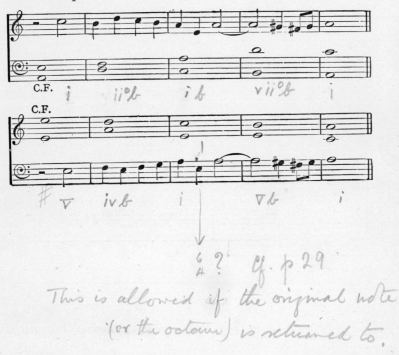

$\frac{6}{4}$? *Cf. p 29*

This is allowed if the original note (or the octave) is returned to.

CHAPTER SEVEN

SIMPLE COUNTERPOINT IN FOUR PARTS

88. When all the voice parts, or all the parts but one, are in the First Species, the exercise is in " simple counterpoint " ; when two or more voice parts are in Second, Third, Fourth or Fifth Species, the exercise is in " combined counterpoint." If the previous chapter (dealing with simple counterpoint in three parts) has been thoroughly mastered, the addition of a fourth part should be comparatively easy, though melodic interest is sometimes difficult to attain.

Example of Third Species simple counterpoint in four parts :—

C.F.

I   vi   V b   I   vii° b   I

Inner part allowed to go by similar motion to a 5th. with any other part. Similarly for 8ve. Also note 5 to 5°.

Avoid all these if possible. Treat the C. F. when an inner part as being prominent like bass or soprano.

CHAPTER EIGHT

COMBINED COUNTERPOINT IN THREE PARTS

89. The many possibilities of combined counterpoint can be only briefly touched upon. We may combine 2nd and 3rd, 2nd and 4th, 2nd and 5th, 3rd and 4th, 3rd and 5th, 4th and 5th, or (most useful of all) two parts in the Fifth Species. The same general principles must be observed in all cases.

90. The parts must not move from 9 to 8 or 7 to 8 :—

91. (i) Notes which are struck together at the beginning of the bar are always concordant, and with very rare exceptions those which are struck together during the remainder of the bar must be concordant. The notes so struck may be harmony notes :—

(ii) Or passing notes :—

92. Discords may be struck when the effect is comparatively harmless :—

4th (1) *unaccented*
(2) *one part by step*
(3) *the other arpeggio*
(4) *perfect*

93. (i) The interval of a perfect 4th may be used when a passing note occurs on the third crotchet in a bar of four crotchets ; but the 4th is best when taken by contrary motion :—

4th (1) *accented*
(2) *resolving by step.*
(3) *perfect*

Two chords in a bar may be freely used, as at (*b*) above ; but here the passing note, occurring at the change of harmony, is not advisable.

(ii) The augmented 4th, or its inversion the diminished 5th, may be used quite freely over a sustained tonic or dominant, provided it is properly resolved :—

94. The second note in an octave leap may often be ignored :—

95. When quavers are used an agreeable effect must be produced between the semibreve, a moving crotchet, and the quavers :—

96. In every instance the sustained note or notes must be carefully considered :—

Not Good.

When this simple rule is ignored, the counterpoint is certain to be ineffective.

97. The harmony may be changed when a suspension is resolved :—

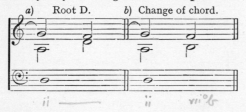

a) Root D.   b) Change of chord.

98. (i) Combined with the change of chord described above a prepared diatonic 7th may be used in any position except the second inversion :—

Root Position.   First Inversion.   Last Inversion.

In each case the notes struck on the first beat are concordant.

(ii) For the Fifth Species all the above may be made florid :

* Some authorities would condemn this as the Tritone. But such progressions should be allowed.

99. (i) In the Fifth Species imitative entries should be used. These may imitate the C.F. either by direct imitation or by inversion :—

(ii) Or the imitation may be on a new figure :—

(iii) The figure

makes an effective start (but see Section 79).

100. Care must be taken to make the two Fifth Species interesting. They must be melodious and have a good range ; the rhythm must be contrasted, and also the movement (by step or by leap). Quavers should not be used too freely ; two groups in a bar, either together or separately, should rarely be used. The parts should sing well individually and the combination should be effective.

(i) When skill has been acquired with the imitative entries the student should try to write the two fifth species parts in canon.

(ii) The Nota Cambiata (see Section 63) may be freely used.

(iii) In four-part florid writing a semibreve is occasionally helpful. This should be tied over into the following bar :—

Some writers insist on the second of two tied notes being either equal to the first or just half the value. But if the note marked * is to be a suspended discord there should be no objection to an ornamental resolution :—

(iv) In combined counterpoint quavers may be taken by leap of an octave :—

(In simple counterpoint students should avoid the above.)

Examples, with two added parts in Fifth Species :

(1) A prepared diatonic 7th.

(2) This is best regarded as an upward suspension, 5 to 6 (root B flat).

(3) Quavers approached by leap of an octave.

(4) This B flat could be suspended ; but see Section 81 (vii).

CHAPTER NINE

LESS REGULAR FORMS OF COUNTERPOINT

SECOND SPECIES IN TRIPLE TIME.

101. (i) Auxiliary notes on the second beat should not be written too freely :—

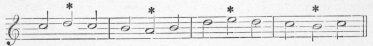

(ii) Arpeggios do not make good counterpoint :—

(iii) The harmony may be changed on either the second or third minim of the bar (see Sections 47 and 60) :—

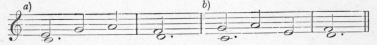

(iv) The Nota Cambiata may be used :—

THIRD SPECIES IN TRIPLE TIME.

102. (i) There are six notes to one of the C.F., and $\frac{3}{2}$ time must be kept in mind :—

(ii) Auxiliary notes should not occur on the accents, but passing notes and the Nota Cambiata may be freely used :—

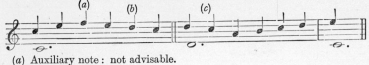

(*a*) Auxiliary note : not advisable.

(*b*) Passing note : good.

(*c*) Nota Cambiata : good.

102 A. Six notes to one are occasionally required in $\frac{6}{8}$ time. Here the safest procedure is to have concords on the first and fourth crotchets. The general effect is like that of the Second Species (Section 101) over repeated notes in the C.F. :—

But some authorities would permit a passing note on the fourth crotchet.

FOURTH SPECIES IN TRIPLE TIME.

103. A suspended discord may resolve on either the second or third minim of the bar :—

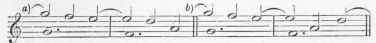

When the first note of the bar is a concord (as in bar one of each of the above examples), the second minim may be a passing note.

FIFTH SPECIES IN TRIPLE TIME.

104. (i) A dotted minim (𝅗𝅥.   𝅘𝅥 𝅘𝅥 𝅘𝅥 or 𝅗𝅥 𝅗𝅥.   𝅘𝅥) should rarely be employed in two parts ; in three parts the effect of the halt would be overcome by the other moving part.

(ii) When the third minim of the bar is preceded by crotchets it must be tied over to the next bar, thus following the ordinary procedure of Fifth Species :—

(iii) Quavers should be avoided :

Examples :—

(a) Many authorities allow such octaves.

CHAPTER TEN

APPLIED COUNTERPOINT

105. In applied counterpoint all the resources of modern harmonies are available. There may be great freedom in the part-writing, but it must always be remembered that the student has to " go through the mill." With certain exceptions the writing of Bach is very scholastic and explainable. We shall give a few opening bars from a number of his works. The Miscellaneous Preludes, Variations (or Partite), Eighteen Chorals, Schübler Chorals, Clavierübung, Orgelbüchlein and Inventions will well reward diligent study ; later the Preludes and Fugues may have attention. The Canto Fermo may be in even notes (crotchets, minims or semibreves) or in florid writing—the latter preferred.

106. The following examples are in two-part writing. At (i) the C.F. is in crotchets, with an occasional elaboration ; the added part, in semiquavers, continues in an instructive manner during the rests in the C.F. :—

CHRIST, DER DU BIST DER HELLE TAG.

(Choral Variations : Var. 2.)

At (ii) the given parts are introductory to the entry of the Chorale in the organ pedals. Regarding the treble part as the C.F., we see how admirably Bach brings in the second part imitatively and then continues in the same style of writing :—

ORGAN PRELUDE ON " WIR CHRISTENLEUT."

(From the Miscellaneous Preludes.)

* Entry of Chorale.

At (iii), still regarding the upper part as the C.F., we have a few preliminary notes in the added part :—

ORGAN PRELUDE ON " WO SOLL ICH FLIEHEN HIN."

(From the Miscellaneous Preludes.)

And at (iv) the parts enter in canon, apart from the preliminary notes in the bass :—

ORGAN PRELUDE ON "WO SOLL ICH FLIEHEN HIN."
(From the Six Schübler Chorale Preludes.)

(v) Against a non-florid Canto Fermo the student should endeavour to use imitative figures, or at least carry on in a connected manner :—

107. In the example at (i) the three parts enter imitatively and continue the given figure. The chorale (on which the introductory figure is based) enters later on the organ pedals, in minims :—

ORGAN PRELUDE ON "VALET WILL ICH DIR GEBEN."

(From the Miscellaneous Preludes.)

etc.

* Entry of chorale in minims.

At bar two of the example at (ii) the C.F. is varied slightly, and the resulting figure is used imitatively in the other parts :—

VARIATION 6, ON "SEI GEGRUSSET."

(From the Chorale Variations.)

etc.

At (iii) the treble and bass are imitative :—

VARIATION 9, ON "SEI GEGRUSSET."
(From the Chorale Variations.)

etc.

108. We now give two examples in which the imitative entries are based on the C.F. :— *(by diminution)*

ORGAN PRELUDE ON "HELFT MIR GOTTES GÜTE PREISEN."
(From the "Orgelbüchlein.")

etc.

PRELUDE ON "DIES SIND DIE HEIL'GEN ZEHN GEBOT'"

(THESE ARE THE HOLY TEN COMMANDMENTS).

(From the "Orgelbüchlein.")

109. Occasionally Bach uses the imitative entries in a still more interesting manner. He introduces the opening phrase of the chorale by a few bars, thus :—

Each subsequent phrase is introduced in this way. We give a skeleton form of the complete prelude :—

"ACH GOTT UND HERR."

(From the "Orgelbüchlein.")

Further examples of this method may be seen in :—

(a) "Aus tiefer Noth," from the "Clavierübung," Part 3.

(b) "Valet will ich dir geben," from the Miscellaneous Chorale Preludes.

(c) "Nun danket alle Gott," from the 18 Chorale Preludes.

ADDITIONAL CANTI FERMI

9.

10.

11.

12.

13.

14.

15.

16.

17.

18.

19.

20.

21.

22.

23.

24.

25.

34.

35.

36.

37.

38.

39.

40.

41.

42.

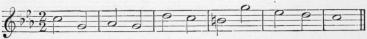

43.

44.

45.

46.

47.

48.

49.

50.

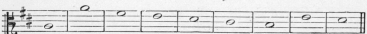

51. Add a treble part to this C.F. :—

52. Add a bass part :—

53. Add a treble part :—

54. Add a treble part :—

55. Add a bass part :—

56. Add a bass part :—

57. Add a treble part :—

58. Add a bass part :—

59. Add a treble part :—

60. Add a treble part :—

61. Add two imitative parts over this bass. (In the original Bach adds two parts in canon, one in contrary motion to the other.)

62. Add two imitative parts above this bass. (In the original Bach adds two parts in canon.)

63. Continue the following for about ten bars, for three voices :—

64. Continue the following for eight bars, for voices :—

65. Continue on these lines for eight bars for the organ. The upper parts may cross freely :—

66. Continue this for eight bars :—

67. Continue this for ten bars, for voices :—

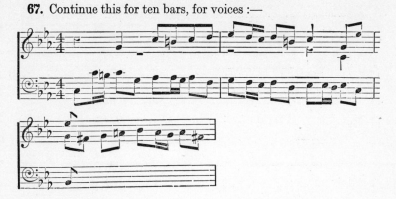

68. Continue the chorale " In dich hab' ich gehoffet, Herr," in the style given :—

69. Continue the chorale " Erstanden ist der Heil'ge Christ " in the style given :—

70. Harmonise the given chorale for organ. Begin with two or three introductory bars based on the opening phrase, and introduce each subsequent phrase with imitative entries :—

INDEX.

The numbers refer to the Sections and not to the Pages.